SPHERE SPUN

Verse By
Jim Gronvold

Also by Jim Gronvold

Back River

Oak Bones

Star Thistle

Pith & Piffle

Word and Mortar

Cogs Turning

SPHERE SPUN

Verse By
Jim Gronvold

Oak Ink Press
2021

ISBN-13: 978-1-7362973-0-8

Book and cover design by Jeremy Thornton
Cover artwork by J. Alan Constant

To order additional copies
Or to contact the author, write:

OAK INK PRESS
oakinkpress@icloud.com
or visit
www.jimgronvold.com

To all the courageous

and kind

people on the frontline

of COVID-contagion

Acknowledgements

With gratitude to *The Lyric* and *The Seventh Quarry,*
Swansea Poetry Magazine: in which the following
poems first appeared:

The Lyric: Listen; Lawn Chair

The Seventh Quarry: 5 Cwmdonkin Drive;
Dylan's Room; Laugharne; Swansea Dylan

I am grateful to Peter Thabit Jones, editor of
The Seventh Quarry Press for publishing my
collection, *Cogs Turning,* in which the following
poems first appeared:

Dragonfly; Arthur's Stone; Presence; Unsung,
What; An Answer; Poetry

Contents

Earth

Our rolling home spins
in an endless expanse

of wheels within wheels
with wheels of their own.

The birthplace of
our existence

a speck afloat
on seas unknown

a drop in an ocean
floating on oceans

where I have felt
stars at my feet

and echoes of you
in my own heartbeat.

Myriad

How many of me
stared at night sky

and wondered at
the numbers of we?

How often a time
caught passing by

held our breath
for moments to be

how long by the sea
that winding stars fly?

Sphere Spun

Frail as we are
beneath the crush

of falling and
flickering stars,

trust the sun
to rise as we spin

on this rare sphere
we share as kin

to wings that ride
turns of season,

fins that glide
swirling tide

and our own
flights of reason.

Hallowed

Sunrise is sacred
to birds of praise.

Sunshine is holy
to faithful flowers.

Sun-prism haloes
glorify showers

and sunsets bless
the passing of days.

All that is ours
was born of the rays

that brighten the
hours
that burn in their
blaze.

This

Moments too
sacred for eternity.

Minutes a sin
to dismiss.

Hours too holy
for ceremony

or futures
no truer than this

for as long as
we find beauty

at the edge of
the endless abyss.

Clarity

Struck by the grace
of the simply seen —

the colors and shapes
of a walk in the wood.

Landscape, seascape,
clouds on a stream.

Wonders that should
be understood

for what they are,
not what we dream.

Risen

Lifted by a breeze
to a wider view

I float on the breath
of heaving hillsides.

Aroma of earth.
A tumbling stream.

Grace descending
not from a dream

of Spring
never ending

but from the blood
of clouds wrung blue

and gathered again
from the risen dew.

Furnace

The sun blesses
as it damns

without feeling
or intention.

That great furnace
heats the sky

that we mistreat
and toxify,

tainting the air
we occupy

with curses of
our own invention.

Keys

From the massive
to the minuscule.

From constellations
to single-cells.

The tiniest thimble
of tide pool

harbors a spark
of deepest sea.

A splinter of bark
in a planted park

carries a key
to the galaxy.

As we, in our
separate shells

carry the fate
of our greater selves.

Ours

We matter to each other
more than the stars

that gave us the
matter that we are.

More than memories
or memoirs.

More than our
favorite fantasies.

More than then or when,
while now can still be ours.

Being

More than the dust
we come to be,

we are the feelings
that moments unfold—

complex creations
of reality—

and not the angels
that we were told

would soar on wings
for eternity.

Nor ghosts of ourselves
in a different mold

forged by forces
of destiny.

Our existence
is the time we hold.

Presence

We live as in
another day.

One to be —
or already known.

But past and future
fall away

when we finally face
the stars alone

or cast a last shadow
on moments met halfway.

Temporary

Morning rises
to midday.

Evening slides
into history.

Vivid moments
will fade away

as minutes and hours
fill their days

with time forever
temporary.

Wishful

What we want to
believe
we usually will

but wishful thinking
is no great skill

and daydreams won't
rescue the time they
kill

but reason can feed
what wishes won't fill.

View

Years are too few
not to watch well.

Stop for the view
whenever you can.

It may not be
the Grand Canyon,

or the blue waters
of Corfu,

but any good
landscape should do.

Try not to look
for more than is there

or what it might
mean to you.

Forget about clues
to some masterplan.

Just watch how
it holds the light

and notice
anything new.

Conjure

If you look for ghosts
in the light of day

when shadows are
little more than shade,

you'll really enjoy
the dead of night

when imagination
may be made afraid

by a whispering tree
or creaky stairway

that tricks the senses
to hear what you fear

and conjures what you
expect to appear.

Loony

Do dogs think they
will live forever

or are they too smart
to act that clever?

I don't guess that geese
get a grip on their grief

by finding relief
in a gander belief.

But I have heard
a few learned loons

wail like wizards
unwound by the moon

expounding on powers
beyond slight of hand

that only they
may understand.

Shazam

Life is too short
for hocus-pokus

or any sort
of mocus scam

that tries to support
some bogus sham

to shock the flock
with flimflam-shazam.

Sleepwalk

The painful fact
of mortality
should inspire
more urgency.

But fantasies
of "Evermore",
that followed us
out of folklore

sing lullabies
of dream belief
that would ignore
a life so brief

while waiting for
eternity,
as promised by
popular prophecy.

Fair Play

Do we need damnation
to know it's wrong
to rape, plunder or kill?

Do we really need rituals
and spiritual manuals
to make fair play habitual?

Do we need a promise
of paradise
to practice simple goodwill?

Gone

Consider "Gone"
to be gone for good.

Not gone somewhere
there is no there

but gone from
being anywhere.

No here and now
or now and then.

No way to feel
a thing again.

If this were
better understood

why wouldn't we live
as well as we could

and treat each other
as well as we should?

Unexpected

You may never
Slide down
depression's
dark hole

or ache with
an anguish
no words
can console.

But poverty
and tragedy
prowl just beyond
our control

and unexpected
events await
as turns of twist-
ed
fate unroll.

Misspeak

Whatever ideals
direct our days

and guide the ways
we treat each other,

chaos may spin
a word away

under the skin
of something we say

when what is heard
was not what's said

or what is written
is not what's read.

Dispute

Attitudes stuck
on a difference

of race, religion
or opinion

may be deeply felt
but not make sense

when frustration
turns to aggression

and anger leads
to violence.

Agreement

Aware of our
shared humanity

and equal
responsibility

to find what we
agree to be fair

we strive to
thwart hostility

or wear the
wounds we tear.

Ground Zero

We trust what
we wish to be true

and defend what
we think we know

right to the edge
of ground zero

stuck on our own
sword-point of view —

armed to the teeth
to die with bravado.

Cannon Fodder

The hell created
by frightened extremes

sheds innocent blood
for the heartless
schemes

of leaders in love
with authority

who sacrifice armies
and citizenry

to tighten their grip
on hierarchy

for the glory
of passing regimes.

Propaganda

Words are more
than what is said

or heard in phrases
that lies repeat.

Speech isn't free
if it can't be read

or is drowned out
by the drumbeat

of heated fear
and blind hatred.

Democracies die
by degrees of deceit

when trust in the truth
is slowly bled.

Rise

Liars rely
on their alibis.

Bullies fear those
they brutalize.

Tyrants refuse
to compromise —

inflicting pain
behind their lies.

But despots will fall
when enough people rise.

Squares

Stuck in the corners
we carry around

it would be wise
to wonder why

we live in squares
while the world is round

and glass horizons
tempt us to fly

beyond the walls
where we are bound

to drift the sky
where dreams are found.

Heap

While innocents suffer
the injustice of need

the ruthless gather
wealth and power.

Markets bless models
of corporate greed

while labor is paid
by the miserly hour

and meager savings
are painfully bled

while the homeless
devour daily dread.

Landfill

Bulldozers stir
a sea of trash

mashing waves
that roll and crash

sparkling with
smashed bits of glass

in a dumpster hash
of chemical swill

buried, but bleeding
beyond the landfill.

Floods

Oceans rise
under our roofs
and flush our rubbish
into warming seas.

Waves spread
poisonous waste
from nuclear plants
and refineries.

The clear results
of policies
that fail to curtail
the pollution
that multiplies
rising catastrophes.

Smoked

Burning paint.
Melting tires.
Toxins taint air
far from their fires.

Days of haze
shade the sun—
seeding lungs
for oblivion.

We spice the smoke
with melted plastics
and baste in our
own synthetics

having stoked the flames
with toxic trash
that can cover towns
with cremation ash.

Blackout

The city drains its veins
of electricity

to slow windblown
conflagrations
that burn towns down
to chimney-bone.

Streets go dark
under soot-rain cloud.

But when the smoke
finally clears,
many more stars
than before appear
and we can see
constellations
that were lost
in the lights
of civilization.

Innocent sparks
afloat on echoes
of farther—far greater—
ancient infernos.

Pandemic

Wading through
oceanic contagion

death floats
the innocent air

as footsteps slip
on the edge of despair

and reckless swimmers
drag rescuers down

while children face storms
where grandparents drown.

Persevere

Emergency
or catastrophe

bring out the best
we try to be

as we together
or in solitude

face tragedy
with fortitude

and do all we can
to persevere

for reasons as many
as life is dear.

A.I.

Robots might rhyme
in the digital future
when programs refined
to write and recite —
by algorithm
and memory byte —
have surgically mined
our literature
for data collection
and word selection
to recombine
selected expressions
into a semblance
of lucid connections.

But we will still
feel what we feel
and live the lines
our own words fill.

Logged Off

In the rare silence
of dark screens

quiet thoughts might
find their voice —

in a gap between
sleeping machines —

and take a chance
to make a choice

without advice
from a smart device

or before big-brother
intervenes.

Rush-Hour Rain

Clutching the wheel.
Following tail-lights.

Sliding with traffic
in a freeway downpour.

Whip-slash wipers
splash steamy glass.

As crashing wakes
drum the door

and a rising shadow
rushes up to pass,

almost forcing me
out of my lane.

I think, tomorrow
I'll take the train.

Winter Thistle

This twisted mass
of tangled twig—

all shriveled stem
and dark decay.

Thorn turned splinter.
Green gone gray.

These withered remains
will shield the sprigs

that fight for ground
when winter recedes

and thistle rejoins
the battle of weeds.

Perch

From a bench
of fallen branch

I watch treetops
wave winter away.

Vultures haunt hillsides.

Hawks call out prey.

Swallows stitch
the sky they tear.

And cool winds gasp
in the warmer air

as I turn with
the churning day

and shed the winter
weight I wear.

Calla Lily

The perfect poise
of a Calla Lily

cradles a grace
of simple beauty

on a silent lilt
of soft lip

open to a curl
at its tapered tip

tilting towards
the mortality

that it bears
with quiet dignity.

Kelp Knots

A snarled mass
of Bull-whip kelp

uprooted by storm
and tossed on land

has withered to leather
on sunburned sand.

Stiff tan stalks
twisted in knots

and dried in tangles
at odd angles

woven into
parched pretzels

no baker's hand
would have planned

nor obedient sun
done on command.

Dunlin Again

Fireworks flying
under the radar.

Silver feather-
explosions of wing

twist in and out
of sight as they swing

left and right
deflecting sunlight.

Their clouds flash
on a watery mirror

and bounce off
each other's reflections

until they drop
in a downpour

of spilling shadows
pecking the shore.

Turf

Beaks flash.
Colors flare.

Hummingbirds joust
over feeder nectar.

One comes near —
stops in midair —

glares at this creature
perched on a chair

and drops a glop
of plop at my feet

as if he meant
to throw down a dare.

Bushtits

A peeping prattle
of feathered flits

seeping through tangles
of twisted oak.

A chattering flock
of chipper Bushtits

on their daily tour
around the block

twirling off twigs
to snack on the fly

and vanish like smoke
tumbling by.

Dusk

A White-tailed Kite
sails the edge of light

between sunset
and hillside shadow.

Catching the glow
its wings ignite

over swallows
herding insects below

as the valley fills
with falling night

and ocean cloud
drifts into halo.

Vultures

A somber clan
of dark capes

perch and stretch
wind-fingered
wingspan

on leafless limbs
in a wafting mist

and rise on air
kissed by a whiff

of the fetid flesh
they can't resist.

Dragonfly

On a park path—
stalking butterflies—

I was targeted
by a dragonfly.

It locked on a spot
between my eyes

for a floating second

before it spun
and drifted away

to find a better
perch than my finger

or maybe to search
for smaller prey.

Hello

If animals spoke
just a word or two

maybe "Hello"
or "How do you do?"

would we all be
vegetarians

or deplorable
vulgarians?

If fish asked us
about our bait

would we engage
in thoughtful debate?

I wonder what words
birds would translate

to communicate
with human herds?

Listen

Learn the wild calls
of human birdsong

in their tangled streets
or watering holes.

Mark the beats
they tend to repeat.

Note higher tones
and lower groans.

The warbles, mumbles
cries and roars.

The chirping chatter,
and cooing patter

singing as
they soar.

Spring

In that moment
when you fit the air

and fill with the ease
of just being there

a familiar breeze
may raise memories

of younger days
that felt as fair.

But passing skies
could never spare

minutes like those,
or these.

Lawn Chair

Leafy Saturday
morning shade

threatens the order
of plans I've made.

Errands and chores
lose priority

over the pull
of gravity—

a force of nature
to be obeyed

before these quiet
moments fade.

October

Facing far hills
under sky we share

I drink the distance
on a deep breath of air.

Summer shimmers
in autumn's glare

while land holds warmth
that breezes spare.

Days like this
will soon be rare

so I memorize
the light with care

and hope the night
will be as fair.

Receding Rain

On the bright side
of passing rain —

in a fresh splash
of sunlight —

horizons have
nowhere to hide.

Mountains reveal
their true height.

Clouds shrink
as winds subside.

Blue skies ignite
the dripping terrain

of rising rock
and sprawling plane.

Bahia Trail

A shade-seeking
sweltering high noon
on the sweat-back trail
winding by the lagoon.

Too dry to whistle
with a rustling breeze
rising through blushing
spindle-bark trees

that tease the path
with dappled oases
awash in the dust
of an arid August.

Foothills

These hills write
The Bay's horizon

with lines that set
the tone of place

and colors that
trace the season.

Clouds pace
the pulse of sky

unrolling scrolls
of scrawled grace

that praise the light
they glorify.

Swansea Seawall

Below the stone walk
where I stand

Sandpipers scutter
between the wall

and the tide crushing in
on Swansea Strand

as I wonder at
the courage of birds

that seem to read
the pulse of sand

to feed at the palm
of the tide's quick hand.

5 Cwmdonkin Drive

(Dylan Thomas' first home.)

Early poems
whisper the nest

where the boy
in his hatching

scratched the dawn
of his quest

and the man
in his fledging

spread the span
of his wings

at the edge of the sky
that his words would sing.

Dylan's Room

You can stand in
the echo shadow
of his spark

by the window
where his words
learned to fly

in the room
that held
dreams of sky

and the door
that led to
doors to the park

where the boy
who grew to
a man of words

borrowed the wings
of birds he knew
and rose on the
beats of his joy.

Swansea Dylan

Long since his
young dog
ceased to bark

the dreams
he dreamt here
left their mark.

Long after pubs
forgave his bills

his fans return
to climb the hill

where he slid
down time
on lines sublime

that seashores
away echo still.

Laugharne, Wales

When the wheeling
rain waned

and sunlight stole
the stage again

we wordy friends stepped
a chatty soft shoe

where a boy skipped
puddles of cobbled cloud

that rippled dribbles
of heavenly tears

spun into laughter
by seagull jeers.

Arthur's Stone

When I first found
the Arthur's Stone,
on that high ground
where it stands alone

I made a sketch,
that I hadn't planned,
and measured the rock
hand over hand.

But, counting out loud,
my voice shifted tone
and I imagined
a mumbling moan

of buried echoes
of long-gone tales,
or a stone held song
of ancient Wales.

Train To London

Layered clouds climb
out of hedgerow pastures

in the moving frames
of windowpanes

speeding past
pastoral pictures

of checkered green
on rolling planes

towards rush-hour crowds
and tidal traffic

where we'll wash up
on curb and brick

to paddle our way
through urban terrain

and come up for air
on a public park lane.

Lancaster Gate

Shrub shaded moss
on a soot spotted wall

at an iron barred gate
to the ambling maze

of bark-armored giants
whose leaf shields fall

on the prim promenades
and paved pathways

of refined nature
heeding protocol.

Rewind

Back over waters
my grandparents crossed

when they were tossed
on the storms of their day

the ship I took
went the other way

past the Statue
of Liberty

to the old world
of our history

where I would
look for yesterday

and learn —in time—
that I could not stay.

Normannerne

I was a king
in a viking movie

for a full film minute
that took two days to shoot.

Danish king Juul,
or "Erik The Lucky."

A courageous leader
of auspicious repute.

My close-up scene —
in a dragon ship battle —

had arrows hit the mast
just hairs from my head.

But my real-life drama
happened hours before

when I led an attack
from ship-to-ship.

With one foot
on each longboat

they slowly began
to float apart.

I teetered between
two drifting hulks —

about to flip
into the bay.

But just as my feet
began to slip

the tide rippled
a fortunate way

and the hulls moved
close enough to leap.

So a stroke of luck
saved my day

but the film itself,
wound up on a shelf.

Roman Candles

I used to enjoy fireworks.
Now I see the smoke and dye
insult an evening sky

and remember my last display —
one snow covered New Year's Eve —
on a farm an ocean away.

When all my rockets were gone,
I held a handful of roman candles

and casually drew wavy haloes
over the scattering shadows
of my suddenly frightened friends.

Their panicked faces flickered
against a flat barn wall

in a sped-up silent film
of flashing shapes fleeing the yard.

It made me laugh so hard
that I lost my grip

and a few flares
backfired into my chest.

Suddenly breathless
and bent by the blow

I saw smoke rising
from my thick wool shirt
and thought that I'd been shot.

But even though I wasn't hurt,
my love of fireworks died on the spot.

Assistens Cemetery, Copenhagen

In that city yard
of ashes and bones
where Kierkegaard
lay not too far
from a monument
for Niels Bohr

I happened to find
forgotten names
stacked in the back
behind a wall—
there to make room
for newer stones—
and I knew what those
evictions meant.

Rest in peace evermore,
but someone needs
to pay the rent.

S.F. Sunday

It's the kind of day
by the bridge-gate bay

when trees play the wind
to a whisper.

Words charm their way
out of a breeze

and you almost hear
skyscrapers purr

as sea-air prowls
deserted alleys

and hilltops scratch
the clouds they stir.

Canadian Lake

I was swimming across
a wilderness lake

with my teenage pals
when the monster struck.

The first bite
hit me on the hip

and sent me flapping
like a mad duck

quacking alarm
to warn my friends.

Then, half-way to shore
it hit me again.

And as I crawled
onto an island

I felt something
pinch my thigh.

An angry wasp
trapped in my trunks.

I slapped it away
with a quick backhand

but only heard laughter
when I yelled "I'm Okay."

Day-Boat

Murray and I
took a full van

of land-stranded,
street-wise, fishermen

from their Boston shelter—
The Pine Street Inn—

for a day of fishing
on a boat out of Lynn.

We left the dock
on an even crawl

but farther out
the sliver of shore

would rise and fall
below the horizon.

I was mesmerized
by the rolling motion

until a crew member
ran to the rail

and spilled his guts
on the heaving ocean.

Then one old joker
from our jolly band

told me I looked
"Crypt-keeper pale"

and that was the straw
that tipped the scale.

But between waves
of seasick eruption

I saw whales
rise and breach.

One even passed
just out of reach

and, I swear, the eye
I saw saw me

which is why
I no longer
drop hooks in the sea.

Street Eddie

He'd polish windows,
cars and doors

leaving abstract streaks
in the stubborn grime.

His tips—at most—
were nickel and dime.

The rags he wore
were ashtray gray

from the dust he wiped
with an old shirt.

His pants were pressed
with the soot and dirt

of a box somewhere
in an alleyway.

But his innocent smile
was what really hurt.

Hector

First in line
for a bed or a meal.

An old prizefighter
battling decline

he could still punch
but not take a hit

and he had a cough
that wouldn't quit

so I found him
a boarding house room
for the winter.

A warm place
with a bit more space.

But his first night there
the building burned down

and that's where my friend
met his hard-fought end.

Uncle Paul

For a few Summers—
before sixty-five—
we'd visit my
great-uncle Paul
on the hospital grounds
of wheelchair parades.

An unsung hero
of World War One,
he was shell-shocked
and silent for decades.

He'd sit and stare—
smoke his Pall Malls—
but never spoke
or seemed to care
whether or not
we were there.

I'd watch him blink
over the top
of newspapers
held up like shields
and wondered if
he was staring
through the loud smoke
of old battlefields.

E.R.

From a gurney
by a wall
in the E.R.

I saw the staff
weave through crises

with the seamless ease
of floating bees

tending to
case after case

with the expertise
of skillful grace

while they tried
to find the bed space

to keep me alive
in their healing hive.

Unsung

The awkward silence
of hesitations
trapped on the tip
of a tied tongue

repeat the fate
of best intentions
learned too late
to tell when young

or bound by age
to old precautions
that hide the hand
of the deeply stung.

Heard

So much to say
in so many words
that could be heard
from the beaks of birds

or pantomime-poet
leafy limbs
scribbling the winds
that hold sway

on whispering hills
of green hymns
where innocent song
is silence's prey.

What?

Is it what we know
or what we feel?

Or, how we feel
about what we know?

And how do we know
what we feel is real?

Or, if what's real
is not what we feel

and the real deal
is not what we know?

An Answer

This is one answer—
the why and how.

The only clue
that life need allow.

These moments few.
This here and now.

Bio

A simple rhymer
of what I see

whose lines
aspire to poetry

inspired by
natural beauty,

the sharp spur
of mortality

and the hope
of our humanity.

Brevity

Moved by words that
ripple their shadows

I strive to write
a tight verse

of simple sounds
that strike and ring

expanding towards
an understanding

of echoes the right
phrase might sing

in plain-spoken praise
of simply being.

Poetry

Natural patterns of sound
that seek or have found
reasons to speak—

to regret or rejoice
in writing or voice —

and make some sense
of experience
before returning to silence.

Speechless

Sometimes silence
is the best way to say
how a walk in the wood
might sound.

It's fine not to find
words to expound
on surroundings
we would portray

in a clever way
far less profound
than the whispers
of a quiet day.

Tumbleweed

The optimism
of tumbleweed

is the patient way
it waits to breed —

trusting the wind
to roll out its seed —

beyond the hole
its roots are buried.

The way a poem
might be carried.